King Goes to School

SCHOOL
King Goes to School
Written by: Sirena Brower

It's been a year since Covid Hit We have to wear mask so we won't get Sick.

The School's are Closed and No one knows when things will go back to like it's supposed.

In front of the computer is where King would sit.

He would often say " This is no fun,
Not even a bit!".

King would day dream about playing with friends.

While counting the hours
until the school day
would end.

Going to school from home
wasn't so bad in a way.

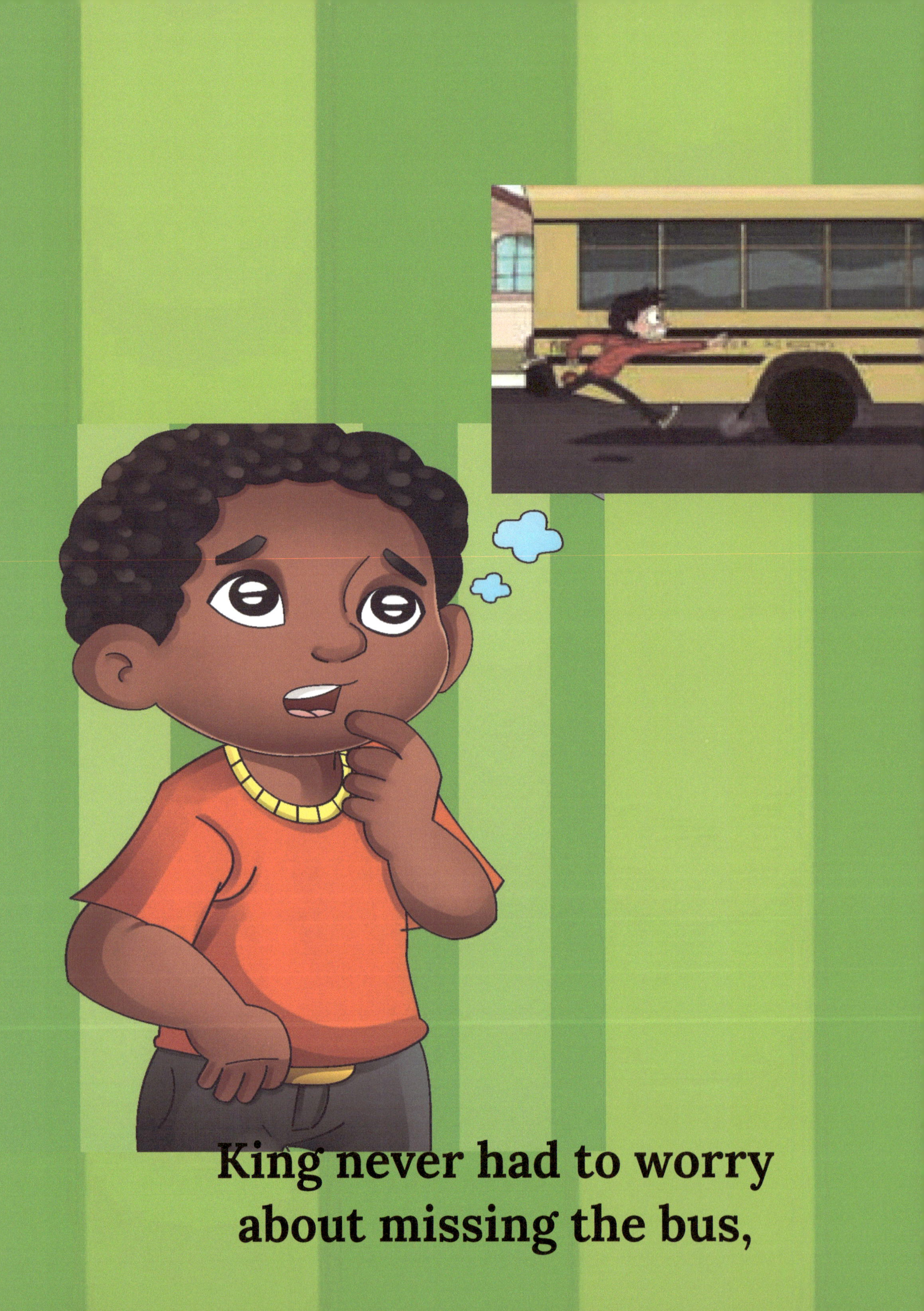

King never had to worry
about missing the bus,

and everyday was Pajama Day!

Every Morning, King logged into Microsoft Teams

Each day he would learn
lots of new things.

He Learned to write the alphabet.

How to count
to 100
and group
objects into sets.

King Learned to spell and write his own name

and he loved to play
matching games.

He learned how to sound out new sight words.

and to think school was boring
was just absurd.

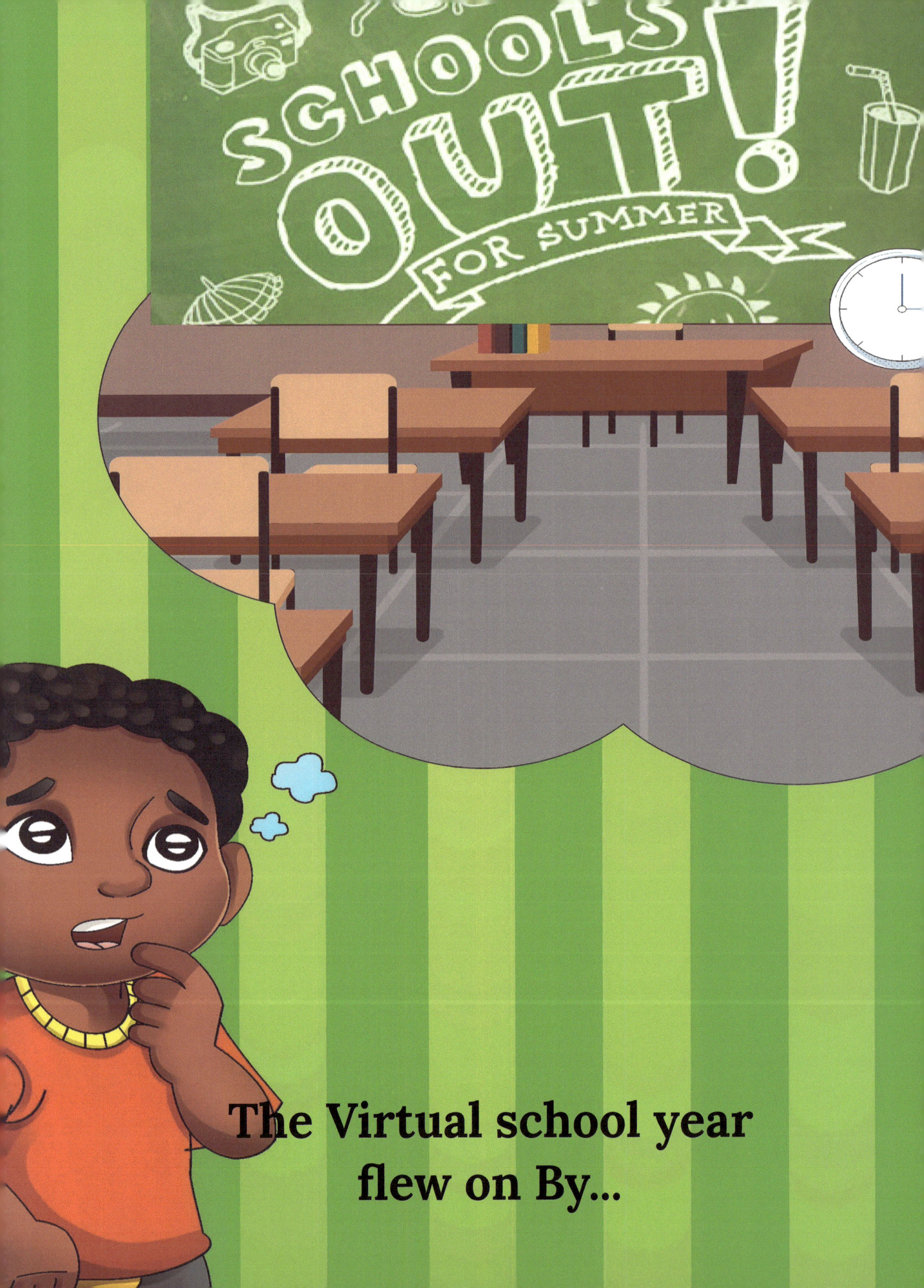

SCHOOL'S OUT!
FOR SUMMER
The Virtual school year
flew on By...

And before you knew it, it
was Summer time.

It Turns out
that Kindergarden wasn't so
boring after all.

But what makes it even better is....

King gets to go to School for
the first time this Fall.

The End.